"... And For Dessert ..."

". . . And For Dessert . . ."

Text and Photography by Ron Adams
with Leslie Kerins Adams
**Recipes and Plate Arrangement
by Thom Wilmoth**

We all think life can be better than it is.

And, it can be. After all, if we didn't want more from life, we would stagnate - live like vegetables. ✎ Fortunately, our desire for better, more interesting ways of living is very much part of us. This desire has brought us out of caves and built a civilization which allows us to live potentially full lives. ✎ Life, for most of us, is relatively comfortable when compared to the life of our ancestors. Yet, for all our progress, we still fail in one thing - the ability to touch one another, the ability to love. ✎ In this, we are each afraid. ✎ Our fear holds us apart, giving us a feeling that something in our love is missing; tenderness, passion, suspense. ✎ We want our lover to tease and tantalize; to be eager, patient, and satisfying. ✎ But fear, and its companion, inhibition, tend to convert what should be beautiful into a rushed, inimaginative, inconsiderate act of NOT loving.

How do we change?
How do we conquer fear? How do we learn to share and give of ourselves and
our senses? ✎ *Tricks and routines are not enough. We must start on a level*
much more basic. Let's blend another elemental need and desire with our need
for love. Perhaps the two together will lead us on. ✎ *It has been*
said, "Man does not live by bread alone." If food is the substance of the body, then
love is the nutrient of the soul. Why not make sharing a meal together part
of the act of love? ✎ *A meal can be prepared carelessly - solely to fill our*
stomachs. But, in the careful hands of a master chef, it can become a
memory to be treasured the rest of our lives. ✎ *So it is with love. What better*
way could we begin to share and give to each other than by
breaking bread together?

The start is simple. It begins with your
decision to have a sensual evening.   If there is any doubt in your mind
whatsoever about wanting a sensual experience, forget the whole idea.   Once
you have made up your mind, you are halfway there. The only real
obstacle is yourself, or at least one part of you . . . your fear.   The
reason most people lead dull lives is obvious: a dull life is a safe life. If you never
open yourself to adventure, you have never given fear a chance to start.
Or, perhaps, to stop.   Our biggest fear is making fools of ourselves. Our
biggest question is always, "What would they think?"   The answer
can be found in ourselves. Would you be insulted if someone really wanted
to love you? Would you be insulted, or excited?   Wouldn't you love
someone who wanted to reach out and touch you?   We think you would.
We don't think anyone would feel you were foolish for wanting
them.   We, all of us, want love. Yet, most of us are afraid of rejection;
so afraid, we close ourselves off into a little island of fearful
desire.   But, what if . . . what if we let go? What if we let our warmth
and desire show? What if, just this once,
you said, "I want you . . .!"

So far, we have talked much

about fear. Frankly, the best way to handle fear is to enjoy it. ✎ That
sounds stupid, but think! What about race drivers? Sky divers? Little kids
on merry-go-rounds? The carnival fun house? All these are scary, aren't
they? Yet, they are some of the things we think of as fun. ✎ A rose's fragrance
and beauty are only an inch or so from its thorns. ✎ So let's enjoy
our fear. After all, one of the prime items in lovemaking is the little tingle
it gives your stomach . . . a tingle very similar to fear.

An acceptable fear comes from the act of not being ordinary. The racer or mountain climber uses that "pit of the stomach" feeling to sharpen reflexes. It keys them to greater awareness . . . they see more, hear more, are more alive. In short, they are more aware of themselves - their senses - their surroundings. They are totally committed to what they are doing and what they are feeling. Isn't that what we want from love? So, our first step is to take ourselves out of the ordinary. After all, we are ready to embark on a new adventure - an adventure that perhaps is even more exciting and rewarding than merely overcoming physical fear. It is an adventure of finding ourselves, of reaching out, of overcoming the hang-ups and inhibitions that have made us a lonely island waiting to be discovered.

Out

Out of the ordinary". What do we mean by that? ✎ The ordinary is what we do all the time. It is what happens to make life dull and wretched. It is doing the same thing in the same way, over and over again. That is ordinary. ✎ Tonight, let's do things differently. ✎ On an ordinary evening, dinner is set just as always. The addition of a few candles doesn't really change anything. ✎ But, do we really have to eat at a table? Or with a knife and fork? Do we really have to use a spoon with soup? ✎ These are things we do in the ordinary way. These are things everyone does. ✎ Why do we have to conform? Wouldn't it be more exciting to sprawl among soft fabrics, curve over deep pillows? Think how sensual it would be to really touch the food, not just with your mouth. ✎ Why not surround yourself with textures, scents, sounds and tastes that excite and give you full range for imagination? If you are not going to be ordinary tonight, then break with the past. The past is dead . . . tonight you are alive.

Let's take just one example . . . clothes.

The first thought is to get rid of them. After all, wearing clothes is what everyone does at dinner. ✍ But, think a bit. Very few people find stark nakedness appealing. There is no mystery, no provocativeness, no challenge. Ah, but touches of you showing! Just a little covered, with promise of more to come . . . that's the way. Nothing is more fascinating than a button undone. ✍ Nakedness is not right. Clothes are too restrictive and binding. But, the cloth feels good on your skin, so, eliminate society's buttons and seams as you do inhibition. ✍ Wrap yourself in fabric. Perhaps a square yard of slinky-feeling material wrapped around and pinned only over one shoulder. Or, perhaps add a wild belt. But, above all, nothing else. Wear only the fabric . . . and your desire.

What have we done so far?

We have taken ourselves out of the traditional setting. We have opened
our minds to different experiences. ✎ We have made ourselves ready to
share a seductive meal . . . a sensual evening. ✎ But, sensual is more than
taste. It is more than the sight of a provocative shoulder. ✎ It is
all of our senses, used and blended. Incense, soft music, perfumes,
textures, glowing lights, warm lips . . . all are part of tonight. ✎ Set your scene
completely. Take the phone off the hook, disconnect the doorbell
and television. Cut off the world. ✎ Tonight is for the two of you.
Tonight is to be savored, enjoyed, uninterrupted.

We all know good food should be savored. Only a glutton devours his food untasted. 🖋 Yet, how often is love rushed? An afterthought to a tiring day. 🖋 Tonight is different. There is no rush. No hurry. 🖋 Dawdle, linger, tease, and tantalize. 🖋 Take your time . . . let it build.

Our

whole purpose is to close out the rest of your life. Tonight nothing matters but feelings, excitement, and love. ✎ No one cares about the weather or what happened at work. There is no reason to talk about these things. ✎ For that matter, there is no reason to talk. ✎ Don't! ✎ Communicate by touches, gestures, glances, and by showing your desires. ✎ An occasional cry of delight is permissible.

The secret of sensual loving is
not to take for yourself. ✎ Give. Give to each other. ✎ Both men and
women are more alike in their desires and pleasures than most of us
realize. ✎ You know what you wish would happen. You know the secret,
wild touches you want. ✎ Give them. ✎ Give the pleasures
of your fantasies. They will drive your love to the same ectasy you want -
and will come back many fold. ✎ Tonight, restrictions are barred.
What better, more intimate way to touch, than to offer or accept a
morsel from your own hand. ✎ Finger bowls are elegant, but wouldn't it
be much more sensual to have a larger bowl filled with warm
scented water to cleanse more than fingers?

No restrictions! No inhibitions!

These are the goals. Their lack opens the floodgates of our senses. But, in truth, some restrictions do apply. ✎ The biggest is not to have too much of any one thing. ✎ Wine is lovely, soft, mellow. It helps lower barriers; gives a warm glow inside, but too much is worse than none at all. In excess it dulls ones responses. Just as too heavy a meal makes us sleepy, lethargic. ✎ Having your back scratched is delightful. But imagine eight solid hours of back scratching in one spot. ✎ Yes, we do have restrictions . . . Sameness, tedium, excess of one thing, all are forbidden.

This is a celebration of loving . . .
a tribute to both of you! ✑ You are each special, out of the ordinary, for
you have chosen to abandon the inhibitions that characterize
so many lives. So, without fear, with nothing but anticipation and
wonder, sit down, clear away the entree; then seductively say
". . . And For Dessert . . ."

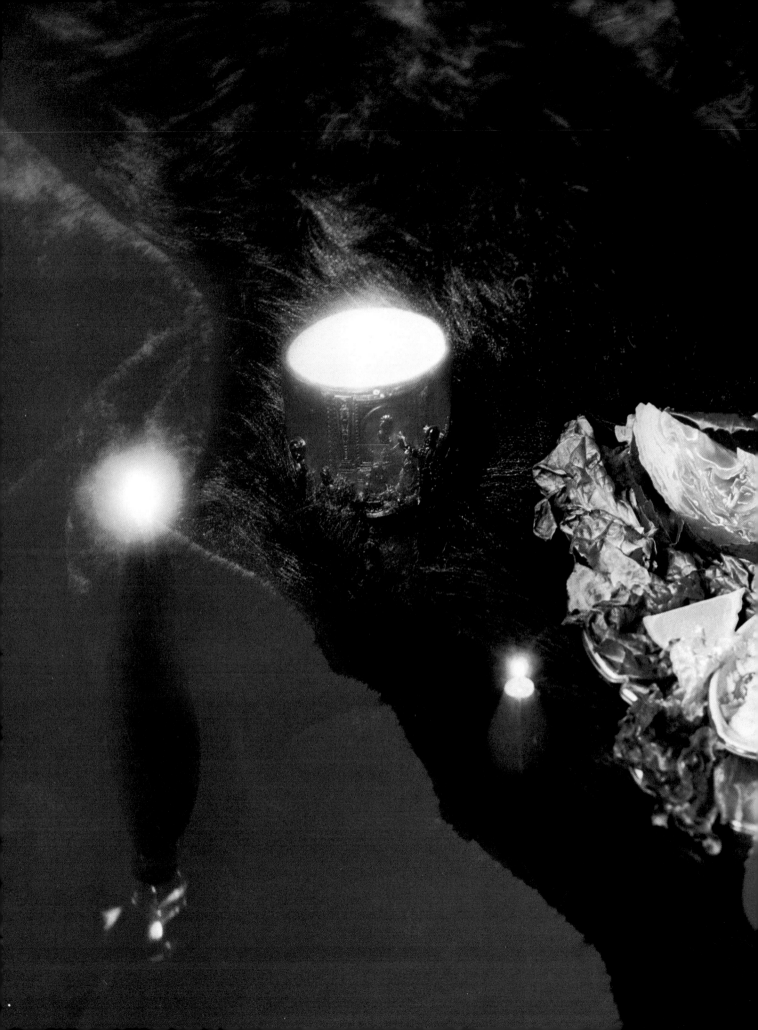

LEGUMES et SOLE POCHEE'

1 lb. Sole
1 Cup White Dry Wine
2 Tbsp. Butter
Dash White Pepper
1/2 Tbsp. Salt
1 1/4 Cup Milk
2 Tbsp. Flour
1 Egg Yolk
1/4 Cup White Dry Wine - Chablis
5 Oz. Asparagus Spears
1/2 Cup Sliced Mushrooms
3 Halved Cherry Tomatoes
1-1/2 Slices of Bread, crumbled
1/4 Cup Parmesan Cheese

Poach Sole in 1 Cup Wine by Simmering (3-5 Minutes).
In a small saucepan start your sauce by melting butter. Add pepper, salt,
milk and flour. A secret to making good sauces is to stir constantly
using a rubber spatula, rather than a whip. Keep stirring until sauce is
thickened. Whip egg yolk frothy and pour a small amount of hot sauce
mixture into egg yolk dish. Stir well. 🍇 The object is to mix some sauce
with eggs, but not enough to cook the yolks into a solid mass. With
constant stirring, pour yolks into rest of sauce. Reheat and add 1/4 cup wine.
Place Sole in individual casserole dishes. Sprinkle with a little salt.
Arrange vegetables on top of fish, then inundate with sauce. Mix
bread crumbs & cheese; sprinkle over sauce. 🍇 Bake at 350 degrees
for 30 minutes. 🍇 Serve on a platter covered with red tipped lettuce
leaves. A couple of cabbage leaves cup lettuce wedges smothered in
french dressing. (Lemon slices add your color and flavor). 🍇 We like the
crunchy type of roll with this dish, to offset the warm moisture of the
sauce covered sole. Chablis wine goes best here.
Furs are fun and tickle all over.

STEAK et LEGUMES

1 lb. Steak - Top Sirloin Cut Thick
2 Tbsp. Butter
3" Onion
1 Green Pepper
1 Cup Mushroom Slices
1 Cup Pineapple Chunks
1 Cup Tomato Wedges
1/4 Cup Sauterne
1/4 Cup Sherry
1 Tsp. Sugar
1/4 Tsp. Seasoning Salt

Broil steak to suit your fancy.
Be sure to leave some color even if you like yours well done. Slice into
1/4 inch strips. 🍇 *In a heavy saucepan melt butter and saute onion*
and green pepper, both cut jullienne style, about 5 minutes or until
tender. Add mushrooms and pineapple. Saute 3 more minutes. Put in rest
of ingredients and cook 2 additional minutes. Drain Juice. 🍇 *Arrange*
steak in serving pan (or platter) and smother with vegetables. 🍇 *Celery*
is cut into 6 inch lengths and filled with Soft Cheese. Use a pastry
bag or aerosol cans to make the filling pretty. Garnish with olives,
parsley, or what you like. 🍇 *We surrounded our nest with the hangy*
down streamers from a party store. They tease and tantalize every
time you move. 🍇 *If you can, try to find some Cabernet Australian Wine.*
It will add to the excitement. It's rich, musky and from "Down Under".

SAUMON A LA SAUCE HOLLANDAISE

2 Eight Ounce Salmon Filets (Boned & Skinned)
1 Lemon Halved
1 Onion Halved
1/4 Cup Mixed Spice
Pinch of Saffron
    Blender Hollandaise Sauce
    3 Egg Yolks
    Juice of 1 Lemon
    Dash Cayanne Pepper
    Pinch of Salt
    1/4 Lb. Butter

Put lemon, onion, spice, and saffron
in large saucepan. Fill with water (allowing room for fish) and bring to boil.
Add Salmon. 🐟 Cook until well done. This should be about 3 minutes
for thinner slices, to 5 minutes for thicker. Do not overcook, unless
you want tough fish. Undercooking is much better. 🐟 For our fast,
delicious Hollendaise Sauce put egg yolks, lemon juice, Cayenne Pepper and
salt into blender. Heat butter 'til hot and bubbling, but not brown.
Turn blender on low and pour butter in slowly and continuously. Blend 10
seconds. Taste. If needed add more lemon juice or salt. 🐟 Surround
a mound of cottage cheese with drained peach slices. Sprinkle cottage cheese
with paprika. 🐟 Garnish plate with endive and lemon wedges.
Hot rolls and soft butter are nice here. 🐟 Claret Wine balances the meal.
Fish Nets, sea shells to hear, and a fisherman's glass balls
make a provocative setting.

CRETETTES

12 Peeled and Veined Shrimp
3 Tbsp. Vegetable Oil
1 Small Can Tomato Sauce
1 Can Tomatoes
1/4 Cup Chopped Celery
1 Small Bell pepper, blanched and cut into 1" squares
3/4 Cup Sliced Onion, dusted with 1 Tbsp. Flour
1/4 Cup Catsup
2 Drops Tabasco

1 Tbsp. Worchestershire
3/4 Cup Brown Sugar
1 Tbsp. Kitchen Bouquet
1 Small Can tiny onions rinsed under cold water
1 Cup Cocktail Tomatoes
1 Can Pineapple Cubes with Syrup
1 Cup Vinegar
2 to 3 Tsp. Soy Sauce

Dust onions with flour. Put in sauce pan
with cold vegetable oil. Cover, bring to simmer for ten minutes. Add celery and
blanched pepper squares, re-cover and continue to simmer for another
ten minutes. 🍇 After adding tomatoes, tomato sauce, tabasco,
Worchestershire, Kitchen Bouquet, and sugar, put sauce pan in 300 degree
oven and bake for 1-1/2 hours. 🍇 The tiny onions, cocktail tomatoes,
pineapple cubes, vinegar and soy sauce are mixed in and placed back
in the oven to bake for a final thirty minutes. 🍇 Make a sumptious mound of
rice on a nicely shaped platter. Hollow out a nest to hold the sauce.
Prepare the shrimp and ring the nest with them. 🍇 Garnish with
avacado slices. 🍇 On another tray center the top of a pineapple
(that's where you got the cubes). Surround with fresh fruit of
different textures, flavors, and colors. 🍇 A rich wine is good to sip as a
counterpoint to the sharp mixture of flavors. 🍇 Eating this meal without
forks or chopsticks is not without mess. But, "Finger Lickin' Good"
is really fun when it's someone else's fingers. 🍇 Dripping sauce
accidentally on a shoulder or tummy is considered fair.
Aren't silks nice on the skin?

BROCHETTES d'HUITRES

1 Jar Oysters
3 Eggs
2 Cups Milk
2 Cups Bread Crumbs
1/4 Lb. Butter
4 Whole Fresh Mushrooms
2 Cups Flour
6 Cherry Tomatoes

Coat oysters in flour. Dip in mixture
of beaten eggs and milk. Roll in bread crumbs. Saute until golden brown.
Dip mushrooms in flour and saute 3 minutes. Arrange
mushrooms, oysters, and fresh cherry tomatoes on skewers. Melon
slices are arranged on a large plate with the Kebobs spread on each
side. Garnish with endive. Arrange various slices of cheese
on another dish, spiced with radishes, celery and / or other crunchy good
things. A side of crackers helps with the cheese. A good Rose' is a
favorite with most people. Exotic Orientals are a sensual setting.
Be langorous and strangely seductive with this one.

POULET AU RIZ

2 Large Breasts of Chicken
1/2 Tsp. Salt
Fresh Ground Black Pepper
1/2 Cup Butter
1 Can Mushroom Slices
1 Tbsp. Grated Onion
1 Cup Whipping Cream
1 Tbsp. Arrowroot
Sherry
Wild Rice

$Skin$ and bone chicken breast.
Season with salt and pepper. Saute in butter about 20 minutes until
rich and brown. 🌰 Remove breasts from pan (but keep breasts hot). In same
pan add mushrooms and onions. Cook 5 minutes, stirring constantly.
Reduce heat, add mixture of cream and arrowroot, again with
constant stirring. Simmer 5 minutes before adding sherry, then 5 more minutes
at the simmer. 🌰 Fill half a platter with cooked rice. Arrange breasts
on rice and smother with sauce. 🌰 Lettuce leaves cover the rest of the
platter with an arrangement of mild and sharp cheese slices. 🌰 For
wine, try Burgundy. 🌰 Served on furs or dark velvets, we put candles
everywhere; scented ones, tall ones, fat ones, big ones, little ones. As
many as you can find. 🌰 Be careful you don't roll on one, and catch on fire.

3 Tbsp. Butter
1/4 Tsp. Dry Mustard
3 Tbsp. Flour
1/4 Tsp. Salt
1/4 Tsp. MSG
Twist Fresh Ground Pepper
1-1/4 Cup Milk
1/2 Tsp. Worchestershire Sauce
3/4 Cup Grated Sharp Cheddar Cheese
2 Tbsp. Sherry
1 Lb. Dungeness Crab
1/2 Cup Sliced Mushrooms
1 Green Pepper

CRABE GRILLE A LA DIABLE

Heat butter in heavy skillet.
Blend in mustard, flour, salt, MSG and pepper. After mixture bubbles, remove
from heat. Very gradually stir in milk and Worchestershire Sauce.
Return to heat, stirring constantly with rubber spatula, until sauce thickens.
Simmer one minute longer. Allow sauce to cool slightly, then stir
in cheese until melted. Add Sherry. Combine cheese sauce with crab
and mushrooms. ❧ Slice rings from cleaned and hollowed bell pepper. Put 3
rings on bottom of each of two ramekins. Cover with crab sauce, sprinkle
with paprika. Bake for 20 minutes at 350 degrees. Decorate with
lemon and parsley. ❧ Sliced cucumbers, green onion, radishes, carrots,
all nestled in a bed of cabbage leaves make a good vegetable side dish.
Try a bowl of salt for dipping or pinching rather than the usual
shaker. ❧ Sparkling Rose is recommended for tingly sipping. ❧ Our room
was trimmed with yards of very soft, slinky, furry, fabric. Pillows were
hidden beneath to give surprising bumps and hollows.

2 8-oz. Portions of Beef Tenderloin
1 Large Baking Potato
1/2 Cup Sour Cream
1 Tbsp. Melted Butter
1 Tbsp. Bacon Bits
1 Tbsp. Chives
1 Tsp. Parmesan Cheese

STEAK FRITES

POULET A LA RUSSE

2 Breasts of Chicken
6 Tbsp. Chilled Sweet Butter
1 Cup Flour
4 Eggs, beaten
1/2 Cup Milk
3 Cups Sifted Fresh Bread Crumbs
1/2 Cup Vegetable Shortening

Bone and skin chicken breasts. Pound flat with cleaver or board. Mold butter into oval shape and wrap with chicken breasts. Carefully seal all edges with toothpicks. 🦃 Dip the stuffed breasts in a mixture of flour, eggs and milk. Roll moist breasts in fresh bread crumbs. Repeat one time, making sure your breasts are fully covered. 🦃 Fry in hot vegetable shortening 8 to 10 minutes or until golden brown. 🦃 Remove toothpicks and serve steaming hot. 🦃 Make a bed of beautiful lettuce leaves on a platter and decorate with asparagus spears. 🦃 Rolls and a tossed salad round out the feast. This time, find a really special, musky beer to serve very cold. Pour with a full foaming head. 🦃 Pick up the breast in your fingers and take a nibble. Your first bite will be an experience.

12 Jumbo Prawns
1 Lemon
1 Onion
1/4 Cup Mixed Spice
13 Cherry Tomatoes
1 Can Smoked Oysters
1 Head Red Tipped Lettuce
1 Can Cooked Shrimp
1/2 Cup Salad Dressing
1/2 Lb. Large Uniform Mushrooms
1 Tbsp. Butter
1 Tsp. Green Onion
1/4 Lb. Chicken Liver, finely chopped
1 Small Package Cream Cheese
1 Tsp. Cognac
1 Pinch Tarragon
Salt and Pepper
Parsley Garnish

SALADE de FRUITS de MER

Broil steak the way you like it.
Bake potato until done . . . 450 degrees for an hour. Cut in half lengthwise,
then hollow each half. Save the skins. Mix potato white with remaining
ingredients. Whip to smoothness. Put in pastry bag then squeeze
back into skins. Re-bake until tops are lightly browned. 🐾 Serve with
rolls, sliced tomatoes and champagne. 🐾 This meal deserves a roaring fire.
Remember - no knives or forks. The weak at heart will cut the meat
to bite size before serving, but tigers tear at it while eyeing future prey.

Peel and de-vein prawns.
Slice prawn halfway through from the back. 🐾 In large saucepan of water,
add half lemon, halved 2-inch onion and mixed spice. Bring to boil.
Cook prawns approximately 5 minutes. 🐾 Hollow out cherry tomatoes.
Stuff with smoked oysters. 🐾 Garnish a large platter with red tipped lettuce
leaves. Tear remaining lettuce into 2-inch squares. Mix with
canned shrimp and salad dressing. Pile neatly in center of platter. 🐾 Alternate
cooked prawns with stuffed tomatoes around edges. 🐾 For stuffed
mushrooms, remove stems and chop them up. Cook the caps in
butter on medium heat for 5 minutes. Remove from saucepan. In the same
pan add chopped stems, chopped green onions and chicken liver.
Cook until liver is nicely browned. Add remaining ingredients and
mix well. Stuff caps with paste. 🐾 Rolls, cognac, grapes and
furs blend well, and delight your senses.

AMUSES-GUEVLE

Banana
Small Pickles
Artichoke Hearts
Pomegranate
Cashews
Jelly Beans
Gum Drops
Cheeses
Grapes
Lollipops
Sausage
Smoked Salmon
Olives
Lunch Meat
Marinated Mushrooms plus anything you like.

6 Eggs
1/4 Cup Whipping Cream
1/2 Cup Crab Legs
1/2 Cup Shrimp
1/4 Cup Celery, chopped fine
1/4 Cup Onion, chopped fine
1/4 Cup Mushroom Pieces
1 Pimiento, chopped fine
3 Tbsp. Butter

Coffee Nudge:
1 Jigger Brandy
1 Jigger Creme de Cocao
1 Jigger Kahlua
Coffee in Large Glass
Mix ingredients and float
whip cream on top.

OMELETTE AUX FRUITS de MER

Preheat oven to 400 degrees.　Mix 6 Eggs with cream, beating vigorously. Combine the rest of the ingredients, saving some crab and shrimp for later. 🍂 Heat butter in omelette pan until it bubbles. Skin top layer off butter and save. Discard rest. Put clarified butter back in pan and heat to smoking. Pour in egg mixture. Cook until outer shell is formed. Sprinkle rest of crab and shrimp on top. Place in oven until omelette rises. For Hors d'oeuvres wrap chicken livers in bacon strips. Skewer with wooden toothpick. Bake 15 minutes at 400 degrees. 🍂 Serve with English Muffins, preserves and Coffee Nudge. 🍂 Although we cap the night with this as breakfast before sleep, it can be served anytime. 🍂 Perfumes and dried flowers make a wild contrast for our senses and tend to bring us awake again.

You

You have broken bread together.
You have made love through sweet wine and let food bring you closer to each other. You have taken simple meals and turned them into a celebration of your senses; an act of love. And in a small way, maybe you and the one you love, learned and saw things in a little different way and have started to break the mighty wall that separates us all from each other. 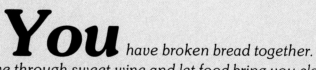 When you share a meal together, make it a night to remember. Be aware of each other and let your senses come alive. Use your ability to see, to touch, to hear, to smell and to taste . . . use it to make yourself more aware and to bring you each closer to each other. For the more you reach out, the more you let in, the wilder, the freer, the more beautiful your life will become. Open your eyes and your heart, your body and your mind. Lay down your fears and open your arms to embrace life. Give your senses the chance to bring you life at it's most precious. There is a whole world of exciting, sensual feelings waiting for you. You can be free like the wind . . . Forget your hang-ups, your fears, your inhibitions, turn down the lights, shut out the world and break bread with someone you love.

*We wish to thank the many people who,
in one way or another, provided inspiration, help and guidance in producing
this book. Special notice is taken of the efforts of Julie
(Sweet Cheeks) Weaver, Merrie LeMay, Lorelei Carlson, Bob Hansen,
and most especially Tiffany and Boy Cat for not eating all
the shrimp prior to shooting.*

Props and Accessories Were Furnished By:
Pier One Imports
Pillow Power
First Northern
Papa John's
Marata Pearl Company
Le Coump's Custom Welding
Pearl Electronics
Napoleans Fine Jewelry

Color Processing by Chromatechnic, Seattle
Type set in Sovenier by Western Typographers, Inc., Seattle
Seperation by Van Dyke, Seattle
Printing and Binding by Kingsport Press, Tenn.